Closing Arguments & The P.E.R.M. Technique

WIN BIG, MORE OFTEN

Jim Garrity

Author of the #1 Amazon.com Best-Selling Book 10,000 Depositions Later: 33 Tips for Taking Superior Depositions

Closing Arguments & The P.E.R.M. Technique

WIN BIG, MORE OFTEN

Jim Garrity

Ross & Rubin, Publishers
New York, New York

Closing Arguments and the P.E.R.M. Technique: Win Big, More Often.

Disclaimer

No part of this publication may be reproduced or transmitted in any form or by any means, mechanical or electronic, including photocopying or recording, or by any information storage and retrieval system, or transmitted by email without permission in writing from the author or publisher.

While all attempts have been made to verify the information provided in this publication, neither the author nor the publisher assumes any responsibility for errors, omissions or contrary interpretations of the subject matter herein.

The views expressed are the personal views and opinions of the author. The reader is responsible for his or her actions.

Adherence to all applicable laws and regulations, including international, federal, state and local governing professional licensing, business practices, advertising and all other aspects of doing business in the United States, Canada, or any other jurisdiction relating to the practice of law is the sole responsibility of the purchaser or reader. The reader should be governed by the rules and regulations pertinent to the jurisdictions in which they practice. Neither the author nor the publisher assumes any responsibility or liability whatsoever on behalf of the purchaser or reader of these materials. Any perceived slight of any individual, organization or culture is purely unintentional.

ISBN: 0998791814
ISBN 13: 9780998791814

DEDICATION

Just a short note of thanks to my mentor, Marie Mattox, who I consider to be not only the greatest trial lawyer currently practicing in the US but also an outstanding teacher, directly and by example, of everything a trial lawyer should be.

About the Author

Jim **Garrity** is a practicing trial lawyer, with a heavy active caseload in federal and state courts in Florida and Georgia. His practice is limited to labor and employment law, with the majority of his cases involving discrimination (race, gender/pregnancy, age, disability, religion, national origin), sexual harassment, FMLA violations, wage and overtime violations and state and federal whistleblower claims.

He has practiced in this area for more than twenty years and has appeared as counsel for plaintiffs in approximately 2,000 lawsuits, roughly split down the middle between state and federal cases.

After graduating law school, he served as a law clerk to the Honorable Daniel T.K. Hurley at the Fourth District Court of Appeal in West Palm Beach, Florida during the Court's 1984-1985 Term. He is admitted to practice before all Florida state courts and in all three Florida federal districts (Northern, Middle, and Southern) and before the Eleventh Circuit Court of Appeals and the United States Supreme Court. He is also admitted to practice in Georgia state courts and the Georgia federal Middle and

Southern Districts. He is a daily commenter in online, lawyer-only practice and strategy forums for Florida and Georgia lawyers.

He is the author of the 2014 Amazon.com #1 best-selling book on trial practice, *10,000 Depositions Later: 33 Tips for Taking Superior Depositions.* He has authored numerous other articles on trial practice, including "Internet Misuse In The Workplace: A Lawyer's Primer," The Florida Bar Journal, Volume LXXII, No. 10 (with former NASA computer scientist Eoghan Casey, M.A.); "The Use Of An Economist In Labor And Employment Disputes: Legal And Practical Considerations," The Florida Bar Journal, Volume LXXIV, No. 11 (with Washington, D.C.-based economist Paul F. White, Ph.D.) ; co-authored "Employment Litigator's Notebook: Twenty Questions About Sworn Statements," Trial Advocate Quarterly, Vol. 20, No. 2; and "Discovery Of An Insurer's Files: Now You See It, Now You Don't," published by the American Bar Association, Tort & Insurance Practice Journal." His article on workplace Internet use was chosen as Article of the Year (and winner of the Barbara M. Saunders Memorial Writing Competition) by the Editorial Board of The Florida Bar from among all feature articles published that year. He has lectured extensively on nearly every major law affecting the workplace, including wage and hour laws, employee rights under the FMLA and ADA, discrimination and harassment, and whistleblower laws. While employed by the Florida Attorney General's Office he was nominated as Civil Trial Lawyer of the Year, from among 400 lawyers agency-wide.

THE SOURCE MATERIAL IN THE DEVELOPMENT OF THE PERM SYSTEM

Pathos

Fear-Arousing and Empathy-Arousing Appeals to Help: The Pathos of Persuasion, Mary Lou Shelton & Ronald W. Rogers, Journal of Applied Social Psychology, Vol. 11, No. 4 (Aug 1981), pp. 366-378

The Thrill Is Gone: Rediscovering Pathos and Style in Debate, James M. Tallmon, paper presented at the 82nd Annual Meeting of the Speech Communication Association, San Diego CA (Nov. 23-26, 1996)

Ethos, Pathos & Legal Audience, Michael Frost, Dickinson Law Review, 99 Dick. L. Rev. 85 Fall 1994

Scherer, K.R., Vocal Affect Expression: A Review and A Model for Future Research, *Psychological Bulletin,* 99, 143-65.

Rochester, S.R. (1973) The Significance of Pauses in Spontaneous Speech, *Journal of Psycholinguistic Research,* 2, 51-81.

Sawoski, Pervez, The Stanislavski System: Growth and Methodology, 2d Ed.

Stanislavski, Constantin, Building A Character, Routledge Imprints (1989)

Eye Contact

Neuroscience and Biobehavioral Reviews 30 (2006) 666–679, Eye movement trajectories and what they tell us Stefan Van der Stigchel *, Martijn Meeter, Jan Theeuwes Department of Cognitive Psychology, Vrije Universiteit, van der Boechorststraat 1,1081 BT, Amsterdam, The Netherlands Received 29 July 2005; received in revised form 13 December 2005; accepted 13 December 2005

Baltazar M, Hazem N, Vilarem E, Beaucousin V, Picq JL, & Conty L (2014). Eye Contact Elicits Bodily Self-Awareness in Human Adults. *Cognition, 133* (1), 120-7

Larsen, Randy J., and Shackelford, Todd K., Gaze Avoidance: Personality and Social Judgments of People Who Avoid Direct Face-To-Face Contact, Department of Psychology, University of Michigan (1996)

Exline, R.V., (1971) Visual Interaction: The Glances of Power and Preference. Nebraska Symposium on Motivation, pp 163-206

Hargreaves, C. P. And Fuller, M. F. (1984) Some Analyses of Data from Eye Contact Studies. British Journal of Social Psychology, 23, 77-82.

Harper, R. G., Wiens, A.N., And Matarazzo, J. D. (1978) *Nonverbal Communication: The State-Of-The-Art.* Chichester: Wiley

Rutter, D.R., Stephenson, G.M., Lazzerini, A.J., Ayling, K and White, P.A. (1977), Eye Contact: A Chance Product of Individual Looking?, British Journal of Social and Clinical Psychology, 16, 191-2.

Ellsworth, P.C., and Ludwig, L.M. (1972) Visual Behavior in Social Interaction, *Journal of Communication*, 22, 375-403.

Goffman, E. (1963) *Behavior in Public Places*, Glencoe: The Free Press

Reid, John E. & Associates, *The Reid Technique of Interviewing and Interrogation* (2000)

Mehrabian, A (1971), Nonverbal Betrayal of Feeling, *Journal of Experimental Research in Personality*, 5, 64-73.

Argyle, M., and Ingham, R. (1972) Gaze, Mutual Gaze and Proximity, *Semiotica* 6, 32-49.

Argyle, E., Communicating by Telephone: Non-Verbal Communication and Cuelessness, 1st Edition, *Pergammon Press*

Gardin, H., Kaplan, K. J., Firestone, I.J., and Cowan, G. A. (1973) Proxemics Effects On Cooperation, Attitude and Approach-Avoidance in A Prisoner's Dilemma Game. *Journal of Personality and Social Psychology*, 27, 13-18.

Rhetorical Questions

Preference for Rhetorical Questions as an Index of Textual Message Effectiveness, Dr. Taiwo Abioye, Ph.D., Covenant University, Vol. 1, No. 11 August 2011

Effects of Rhetorical Questions On Persuasion: A Cognitive Response Analysis, Richard E. Petty & John T. Cacioppo, Journal of Personality and Social Psychology, Vol. 40, No. 3 (1981)

Rhetorical Question Use and Resistance to Persuasion: And Attitude Strength Analysis, Kevin L. Blankenship, Journal of Language and Social Psychology, Vol. 25, No. 2 (June 2006)

You Call That A Rhetorical Question?: Forms And Functions Of Rhetorical Questions In Conversation, Jane Frank, Journal of Pragmatics, Vol. 14, Issue 5, October 1990, pp. 723-738

Effects of the use of introductory rhetorical questions versus statements on information processing. Burnkrant, Robert E.; Howard, Daniel J., Journal of Personality and Social Psychology, Vol 47(6), Dec 1984, 1218-1230.

Effects Of Involvement On Persuasion: A Meta-Analysis. Johnson, Blair T.; Eagly, Alice H., Psychological Bulletin, Vol 106(2), Sep 1989, 290-314.

Deriving The Interpretation Of Rhetorical Questions, Chung-Hye Han, University of Pennsylvania (paper)

Examining The Target Of Receiver Elaborations: Rhetorical Question Effects On Source Processing And Persuasion, John Swasy & James M. Munch, Journal of Consumer Research (Oxford University Press), Vol. 11, No. 4 (March 1085), pp. 877-886.

A Typology Of Rhetorical Questions, Russell Lee-Goldman, Syntax and Semantics Circle, University of California at Berkeley (Feb 2006).

The Meaning Of Questions, Richard A. Hudson, Language, Vol. 51, No. 1 (March 1975)

The Syntax of Negation, Haegeman, Cambridge University Press, Cambridge (1995).

Negative Polarity and Grammatical Representation, Linebarger, M.C., Linguistics and Philosophy 10.3, pp. 325-387.

Metaphors

Metaphor Processing, Psychology Of, Dedre Genter & Brian Bowdle, Northwestern University Press

Grothe, Dr. Mandy, I Never Metaphor I Didn't Like, Collins Imprints, HarperCollins Publishers

Charteris-Black, Jonathan, Politicians and Rhetoric: The Persuasive Power of Metaphor, Palgrave MacMillan/St. Martins Press LLC (2011)

Geary, James, I Is an Other: The Secret Life of Metaphor and How It Shapes the Way We See the World, Harper Perennial – Reprint Edition (2012)

Thibodeau PH, Boroditsky L, Metaphors We Think With: The Role of Metaphor in Reasoning. PLoS ONE (2011)

Sommer, Elyse & Weiss, Dorrie, Metaphor Dictionary; Visible Ink Press; Reissue edition (August 1, 2001)

Nordquist, Richard, Metaphor: A Practical Introduction by Zoltan Kovecses (Oxford University Press, 2002)

Klein, Brennan, 5 Studies: The Ubiquity of Metaphor (2013)

Guo, Song, Metaphor Studies from the Perspective of Critical Discourse Analysis: A Case Study of Business Acquisition, School of Foreign Languages, Tianjin University of Commerce, China Theory and Practice in Language Studies, Vol. 3, No. 3, (March 2013)

Owen, Nick, More Magic of Metaphor: Stories for Leaders, Influencers, Motivators and Spiral Dynamics Wizards, Crown House Publishing (2004)

Ortony, Andrew: Metaphor and Thought, Cambridge University Press (1993)

Www.MetaphorObservatory.com

Preface

This is a practitioner's guide. It is short, easy to follow and easy to use immediately. It is based on proven psychological principles for persuasion.

Of all the discrete elements of a trial, closing argument, or summation as it is called in some jurisdictions, is the component most often constructed on the fly. The pace of jury trials is uneven, and the moment for closing can arrive with little notice. "Organized closing argument" is as much an oxymoron as "reasonable attorneys' fees" and "literal interpretation." Closings often begin immediately after the close of the evidence, which is really the first time lawyers know what is or is not evidence. Even arguments written just before the last witness testifies can suffer a disconnect with the evidence presented to the jury.

So while closings are a powerful chance to win the case, the moment is often wasted, because of disorganization and because of a core misunderstanding about the task.

Traditional descriptions of summations describe them as the stage where lawyers review the evidence. The better description is "your only opportunity for powerful first-person persuasion using scientifically-proven compliance techniques." This is the foundation for the PERM system.

A detailed review of the evidence during closing is unnecessary. Juries are smart. They listen. Regurgitation wastes your time and theirs. Some review of your most potent evidence is essential, *but you must be singularly focused on persuading the jury to answer the verdict form exactly as you need.* If your case was presented as you intended, it is not necessary to press rewind and replay. All you need is a subset of the evidence – your highlight reel – and the powerful, proven techniques of persuasion. Closing arguments are the time to connect, to speak from the heart, to hit one home run after another. You spent the entire trial hitting singles and doubles. Don't do it again. It's home run time.

Every point you make in closing must be a home run. If your closing arguments last an hour, you are hitting singles. No one has an hour's worth of true home run points to make, one after another. Thirty minutes are plenty in nearly all cases. Twenty may be enough. If you're hitting home runs for twenty solid minutes in front of any jury in the US, you're going to win. That would be an extremely strong case.

Experienced federal and state judges know the closing argument is a qualitative, not quantitative, game. In other words, it isn't the length but the quality of your argument that will win cases. Lawyers confuse length and strength. A long closing argument is not the same as a strong one. It can suggest the opposite. A terrible hour-long movie will never beat a great five-minute one.

My strength as a trial lawyer has been to disassemble the trial process, reverse-engineer its components and find out what can be done to reinvent these components to sharply improve results. I have done this in the context of depositions, the summary judgment process, and in several others. I once wrote a short paper analyzing the federal rules, for example, to show lawyers how they could file motions of virtually any length, using novel interpretations to essentially skirt page limits. My approach allowed for near-limitless expansions in page length. Need fifty more pages? No sweat. A hundred? You bet. Some courts have abandoned page limits in favor of word limits to halt this kind of page-length gaming, but my approach would work all the same by allowing equally near-limitless word counts. The "flaws" allowing this are built into the fabric of the rules and would probably survive all but a complete rewrite. In the end, I decided against publishing the guide because I felt it wouldn't gain me any friends on the federal bench and it did not serve the interests of lawyers. Longer is rarely better than shorter. I've often thought that if I were a high school teacher, I would restrict writing assignments to fifty words. Writing effectively with brevity is far harder than writing without limit.

The PERM system is my contribution to the art of closing arguments. It is simple, intuitive and can be presented effectively with little prep time. And these aren't the side benefits of the PERM system. They are the reason it exists. It is easy to remember, does not rely on (and in fact discourages) notes, and is based on four of the most powerful techniques for human persuasion known to science.

The four PERM principles draw heavily on persuasion methods used for more than a century. Advertising executives, corporate marketers, actors and actresses, politicians and governments all make active use of them. Indeed, leaders in these fields sponsored much of the research, and they rely on it heavily. They also happen to use a far broader range of persuasion and compliance techniques, but most are not permissible in court under substantive and procedural rules or professional codes of ethics. They might be fine for selling cars or alcohol, or for persuading people to donate money to charitable causes, but not in our court system. The four PERM components are every bit as powerful as the techniques that cannot be used in court. They're just different. They work when the audience to be persuaded cannot talk back, must make a decision quickly and isn't personally affected by their "purchasing decision" (meaning a verdict for or against you). The PERM system is designed for use in a highly-restricted, closed world – one where the buyers cannot gather any information on their own. They can only make decisions based on what they are given. This is the closing argument phase of a US jury trial.

For two years leading up to the publication of this book I dug into academic and psychological research, some of which is freely available online and some of which is available only for purchase because of the limited market for their specialized data. In researching the science of persuasion, I saw that experts in this field had studied the elements of persuasion at a granular level. What works? And, why? There is a wealth of advanced research, most of which I never even heard of before. Nor was I aware of the incredible scientific principles behind it. Some studies zero in on and analyze the elements of the most deeply-moving conversations we have in our lives: matters of life, death, pain, suffering, joy, marriage, divorce, finances, children and career.

Researchers in the studies asked two questions, subject matter aside.

First, what are the discrete elements of these conversations? What is it about the force of such conversations that can be separated out from the subject matter at hand? What physical mannerisms or linguistic techniques do people consistently use when speaking about matters of grave important that is separate and distinct from the subject at hand? What are they *intuitively* doing in these conversations, across all racial, age and gender spectrums, that signals the highest levels of truthfulness and gravity in their behavior?

Second, the researchers asked, which of those discrete elements are reproducible and can be used in other settings with equal force to persuade?

The answer to these two questions led to this book.

As I worked through the research, I saw four techniques surface over and again that meet the strict evidentiary, ethical and procedural standards for trials. "PERM" is simply an easy-to-remember acronym for those techniques. I then began experimenting with this system and found it to be a complete game-changer for winning verdicts. Best of all, it's easy to use, remember and assemble on the fly - even if you've got just minutes between the close of evidence and the start of summation. In other words, it works, and it works spectacularly.

Questions about this system can be sent to me through Josh Siskind, my publisher's Director of Marketing, at JoshSiskind@rossandrubin.com. We'll also add you to our mailing list to alert you of new publications of interest to you. You'll receive no more than four emails a year this way (and usually no more than one or two). Thank you again. I welcome your feedback.

Jim Garrity
c/o Ross and Rubin, Publishers
New York, New York

INTRODUCTION

I have long thought, in trying cases against the nation's best trial lawyers, that they fell short in presenting closing arguments. They worked from disorganized, hastily-written or edited notes. They stumbled. They repeated themselves. They said things that I suspected they didn't mean to say. Some spoke coldly and mechanically as if they did not believe their own words. They seemed uncomfortable looking at the jury. Their notes seemed to be their safe place, so they spent most of their time looking at the notes, not the jury.

None used a system or framework to present a closing argument. Their presentations were ad hoc. Frankly, I understand that law school curriculums poorly train us all for trial work. The curriculum is too broad. Programs of study are based on the notion that being well-rounded is more important than being ready to practice, so they teach principles most of us will never use. The cost of this breadth is depth. We know a little about a lot, and the result is that we launch as jacks of all trades and masters of none.

Courses on persuasion, memorization, and acting would make us vastly better trial lawyers. Most litigators could learn a great deal from advertising agencies, for example, or from professional actors, about the science of persuasion. But there is no such occupational cross-pollination. So we begin our careers believing-without any training about scientifically-proven principles of persuasion - that juries decide based on the evidence. It doesn't work that way. Your jurors have been heavily conditioned throughout life, and through daily exposure to sophisticated compliance techniques, to make even life-changing decisions based on <u>how</u> a message or decision is presented. Persuasion and authenticity have scientific underpinnings just like engineering or physics. That we don't know them doesn't mean they don't exist. You might be messaging the jury in a way that compliance professionals from advertising or political fields have trained your audience to reject as unworthy of belief. Sometimes outcomes are because of a lack of information, but the ones lacking the information might be us, not the jury.

Worse, we have become poor memorizers. So we rely on notes, which are terrible barriers to effective communication. We use GPS to find our way and no longer remember how to get anywhere. We use calculators for math. And we use the Internet for everything else. The average person, including the average lawyer, no longer needs to remember anything. This is why most lawyers rely heavily on notes during closing. They have to. They have no memorization skills.

I set out to find a short, simple system for trial lawyers that can be used to make powerful closing arguments without memorization, and that specifically incorporates science-based compliance techniques. My goal was to develop a method anyone can use in any jury trial. So it had to meet several criteria. It had to be:

1. Easy to learn, regardless of experience level.
2. Easy to use, regardless of experience level.
3. Compliant with all procedural, substantive and ethical rules.
4. Effective in every kind of case.
5. Effective for both plaintiffs and defendants.
6. Effective with every kind of juror, regardless of race, age, gender or other demographic.
7. Effective without notes.

PERM meets these criteria. It works perfectly even on short notice, when a judge forces you into closing as soon as the presentation of evidence is done. In these courtrooms, there's no going home that night to craft a powerful closing argument. It's show time. In one recent federal trial, the defendant rested its case, and the judge immediately told the jury we would begin closing arguments. There was to be no break. Even in this setting, I was able to give a powerful summation from the top of my head, using my "highlight reel" set of exhibits, because I used the PERM system exactly as I designed for others.

As I will discuss it shortly, the PERM elements are so easy to use they can all be used at one time - even in a single sentence. Used systematically, they will dramatically change your success rate in trial. Some of the most powerful speakers in history - Barack Obama, Ronald Reagan, Martin Luther King, Margaret Thatcher, to name a few - used or use these techniques. This is bolstered by research by Jonathan Charteris-Black, a linguistics professor at the University of West England and a world-renowned expert on persuasion. He analyzed the linguistic content of these leaders in published speeches over the course of their careers. In studying Reagan and Obama in particular - both masters at persuading ordinary people - he found that both presidents used one powerful technique in the PERM system at a rate *more than double that of other world leaders.* It was clear their use of compliance principles was both intentional and extremely effective. (You can find more than one hundred of President Obama's speeches, in full-text, audio, and video at AmericanRhetoric.com. This excellent site has more than 5,000 speeches in multiple formats, all illustrating the use of various PERM elements. I highly recommend this award-winning collection.)

PERM works for very experienced lawyers and brand new ones. Anyone can present spectacular closing arguments using PERM and with very little preparation time. The techniques hit juries at an intuitive level and do not require heavy-handed or over-the-top styles. Some lawyers that I asked to try PERM, and to help me refine it, told me they felt it works precisely because it does not require heavy preparation. Over-engineered summations are the antithesis of the PERM system. They are also the antithesis of persuasion.

If you are the lead lawyer on the case, you already know the facts from top to bottom. You are first-chair because of your knowledge. You don't need screenwriting software or the schizophrenic input of well-meaning colleagues. You don't need to map out arguments and sub-arguments. All you need is your working familiarity with the facts, a handful of your best exhibits, and the PERM system. PERM simplifies your work. Think of it as a quality-control device - a simple and methodical framework for closings. That's what it does. It simplifies.

How do jurors react to the PERM system? Consider the following comments from the jury foreperson in one of my recent federal trials. She called me the day after I won a verdict to share her thoughts about my closing argument. The specific court where

I tried this case has rules that forbid lawyers from contacting jurors, so I was fortunate she decided to reach out and share her thoughts. Here's what the foreperson said about my closing:

> *"I have to tell you….that was one of the most moving experiences I have ever been through….I had no idea a lawyer could be such a great advocate for someone and at the same time show such compassion and kindness and authority. I have never seen it. I was just honored and humbled to be part of it…very powerful, very moving…It was your belief in the righteousness of the situation."*

I was deeply honored by her comments, but I thought nothing of them in a general sense because they simply confirmed the effectiveness of the PERM technique. This is precisely the kind of reaction it generates.

The Four Components of PERM

Here are the four elements, listed not by importance but in an order solely to create the easy-to-remember acronym PERM:

Pathos (Passion)
Eye Contact
Rhetorical questions
Metaphors

These are the four elements of verbal and visual persuasion that psychological and linguistic studies have proven over many decades (1) have the greatest impact in gaining compliance and (2) meet all standards for use in closing arguments in US jury trials.

Pathos or Passion as used in PERM refers to your open display of deep commitment to your points. It is classic *pathos* as defined by Aristotle – the use of emotions that have no essential linkage to the issue. In other words, the display of passion does not necessarily have any inherent connection with the point being made. It is the use of emotion as a tool to persuade – the arousal of emotion in the jury to trigger the outcome you desire. It gains compliance by conveying that your points are gravely serious, that you deeply believe them, and that you deserve to win because you are so clearly right.

Eye contact is integral to PERM for the dual purposes of bonding with the jury and of regulating your argument. First, eye contact creates a bond, a connection, that does not exist when we read an argument from notes. Lawyers who read their argument are missing a valuable opportunity. Eye contact, properly made (and I outline in details the do's and don'ts in this book for eye contact with jurors), builds a powerful personal connection – even more so if your opponent shies away from it. Second, eye contact serves a valuable regulation function. It provides visual feedback, which in turn allows you to adjust on the fly. Visual feedback – nods of agreement, raised eyebrows, slight smiles, head shakes of disagreement, the return of eye contact by a juror or the avoidance of it – is useful for deciding whether to dial your intensity up or down, for deciding whether to spend more time or less on a specific point, and for gauging how many of the jurors are likely to vote your way. You might decide to initiate, or avoid, eleventh-hour settlement talks based on this feedback.

Rhetorical questions are integral to the PERM system for one reason: They are as close to an actual conversation you can have with your jury. Rhetorical questions force jurors to engage with you. The jurors will answer your questions, albeit silently, but that is good enough. A century of psychological research shows that it is nearly impossible for a passive listener to avoid answering a rhetorical question. This tool, therefore, is perfect for jury arguments because it is a real and direct engagement with the mind of every juror. Framed correctly, rhetorical questions compel the jury to agree with you, and to disagree with your adversary. There is also credible scientific research that rhetorical questions are a powerful way to engage audiences who otherwise perceive a dispute as irrelevant to them. In other words, they successfully increase the interest of decision-makers who are deciding *someone else's dispute.* Studies show that when listeners see the outcome as unimportant to them on a personal level, their mental engagement drops sharply. Those same studies show that personal engagement by disaffected audiences rises sharply, however, when rhetorical question are used.

Metaphors, the final element of PERM, are verbal shortcuts used by compliance professionals to associate a listener's existing belief to the desired point. In the context of the closing argument, you'll use them to tie your key points to beliefs the jurors already hold true. Metaphors build on existing juror beliefs about a matter, making it far easier to persuade the jury than if you construct arguments from scratch. You will use concepts the jury already accepts as true as the vehicles for your message, in effect using them to carry your client's position across the finish line. Metaphors can be used to positively or negatively paint an opposing party or witness.

Ordinary people have conversations every day that intuitively encompasses PERM. The question, then, is, if people intuitively use PERM components when everything is on the line - in their personal and important conversations - why don't lawyers? The answer derives in part from the way we are taught in law school. We are minutiae-dwellers. We love the mundane, the technical, and the procedural. We are trained to avoid reacting emotionally because (we are told) that is how clients react, and that is why clients need lawyers.

As lawyers, we also worry about our reputation, and about acting more like a client than a lawyer. Emotional reactions are disfavored. Logic rules. We do not want to seem "too" anything: "too" aggressive, "too over the top," "too close to the edge" of zealous advocacy. We get buried in details. By the time we reach a courtroom, we have over-engineered everything, and by that I mean over-prepared. We try to control for so many possibilities that our case becomes burdened with complexity. Lines of attack and defense become weakened, not strengthened, when we over-engineer. This is a fundamental problem in closing arguments. Lawyers feel the need to address every point for fear the point they omit is the one the jury should have heard.

But this is unnecessary. Your jurors already heard the evidence. They were paying attention. They get it. They do not need to hear it again. The time for presenting evidence has passed. Now is the time for persuasion – for simple, passionate persuasion. You must appear authentic, sincere and natural, without pretense or artifice. You must appear intentional, not accidental. If you are not sure what this means, think back to the deeply moving conversation topics we spoke about earlier – life, death, injury to a loved one, children, the loss of a career, perhaps even marital infidelity. Close your eyes and imagine those conversations. They are entirely unscripted. Yet they are all driven by passion, eye contact, and almost always involve invocations of rhetorical questions and metaphors.

We all instinctively use these persuasion tools in high-stakes conversations because we are hard-wired to convey truth, sincerity, and depth of belief. We are also hard-wired to respond more favorably to arguments presented this way. We are more likely to say yes if a message is conveyed with indicators of truthfulness, such as eye contact and deep passion. We are also more likely to say yes if we are invested in the dialogue, and if the message is supported by beliefs we already hold true. So the PERM system provides the perfect transportation system for your content.

PERM's powerful techniques are used on a daily basis. Where? In homes, in offices, in cars, on baseball fields, in schools and everywhere else ordinary people have disputes of great importance. Imagine a mother whose child has just been injured because of a school's negligence. Her conversation with the school principal will be deeply powerful, and free of notes. Imagine an employee who has just lost his job and is pleading for a second chance. Imagine the conversation between a married couple when the marriage is coming to an end. These deeply emotional moments inherently draw on every one of PERM's techniques: *pathos*, eye contact, rhetorical questions, and metaphors. All four show up in our most powerful, passionate and deeply personal moments. As one spouse approaches the other for the first time about divorce, she asks, with deep passion and conviction, *"How did we spend so many years on this journey, only to find ourselves so far apart and headed down such different paths?* In that single sentence, we find deep pathos/passion, the metaphor of the journey, a very difficult rhetorical question, and, to be sure, eye contact. There is no script, but the framework makes the message content deeply moving.

PERM operates on the premise that because the jury heard the evidence already, and quite likely did so with considerable repetition because we wanted to make sure they "got it," you will not be regurgitating it again *en masse*. You will be striking fatal blows during closing because your content will be sharply refined and wrapped in a framework your jurors are trained to see as authentic and worthy of acceptance, based on their own views of life. PERM reduces closing to its necessary elements. It is aggressively minimalist. Its core principle is that you must strip your case down to its essential qualities to achieve simplicity. Choose your key points. Choose a subset of your best documentary evidence. And then talk to your jury as if your life, your career, and your family depend on it. Speak with the powerful intensity of your client's personal deep feelings. Intensity and simplicity are the heart and soul of PERM.

The Creation of the PERM System

I reviewed more than forty published studies and articles in the field of psychology, psychiatry, and linguistics about techniques of persuasion. Some of the works I studied are listed in the resource index at the beginning of this book to allow you to review them on your own if you wish. These studies involve deep analyses about how our brains process and use information to form beliefs.

I've wondered why these principles aren't taught in law schools, or at least in trial practice courses and seminars. Trial lawyers, like advertising creatives and salespeople, are what research psychologists refer to as "compliance professionals." We are in the business of selling through persuasion. Courtrooms are compliance settings, every bit the same as car dealerships, retail selling floors, and restaurants. Everything we do involves and depends on the ability to persuade others to buy what we are selling.

Yet there are no courses that teach lawyers about the role of cognitive functions - reasoning, memory, attention and language – in persuasion. These cerebral functions are our funnels for earning. They help us determine what we "know." But law schools do not teach this. I reviewed the course titles and descriptions for twenty-five law schools at random, ranging from the top Ivy League schools to a sampling of law schools whose graduates are not permitted to practice outside the state where their law school is located. None offer courses on the science behind persuasion.

Nor is the average litigator taught about how people use learning shortcuts, which are what juries use to form opinions and take sides swiftly. Those shortcuts – academic psychologists call them "judgmental heuristics" – are the foundation for the decision-making process juries use to form judgments and make decisions. These are mental shortcuts that allow us to zero in on one aspect of a complex problem and ignore others. Most people use the phrase "rule of thumb" to describe what compliance scientists refer to as a heuristic. If you routinely avoid eggs and poultry products when there is an outbreak of salmonella, you are using a heuristic or rule of thumb for dealing with that problem. You don't research the likelihood that a specific piece of chicken at your grocery might be infected. You just avoid all chicken products for a while. That is a heuristic or rule of thumb. Juries do the same thing for every piece of information they hear. They will use their own rules of thumb in deciding what your evidence means. Trial lawyers who present evidence - and think the jury accepts it for what it is - probably lose far more trials than they should. If you have twelve jurors, you must consciously appreciate that twelve different sets of heuristics are in play.

The PERM system works exceedingly well because it uses four major heuristics that virtually all humans use to judge right and wrong. This is why your message will become far more powerful. Your jurors, regardless of background, education and life experiences, are hard-wired to accept these heuristics as deeply-reliable indicators of a message they should accept as true:

- ***Pathos*** - the presentation of your closing argument with a deep passion - is a heuristic or shortcut the research shows is universally accepted as a gauge of the depth of belief, seriousness, and sincerity. You are more likely to believe a person speaking on a topic with great passion than someone who says the same thing in a neutral affect. *Pathos* is a scientifically-proven tool of persuasion. The greatest orators of all time use it. It is why they are considered great orators. It isn't the subject matter that drives *pathos* in your closing. It is you. You could be arguing about the length of ceiling fan blades. It does not matter. *Pathos* sells. *Pathos* wins.

- ***Eye contact*** is another universal major heuristic or shortcut used to judge and make important decisions. Research shows the target of an argument is vastly more likely to believe you if you maintain steady eye contact than if you do not. Unfortunately, I see even very experienced trial lawyers reading from prepared notes during closing argument. I do empathize. Trials are high-stakes events. We can't afford to overlook an important point. But notes are like pesky toddlers. They demand attention. They want you to look at them, not the jury. And yet it is the jury, not your notes, that will decide the outcome. In this book I suggest a simple and effective technique for weaning yourself from notes, using admitted exhibits as an alternative to notes. You will already be deeply familiar with the exhibits and can speak freely about them. This approach allows you to directly talk with passion about the key issues without a single note.

1. ***Rhetorical questions*** are a major heuristic for accepting the truth of a message. One major study showed rhetorical questions are the single-most effective linguistic tool for getting engagement from an audience that has no personal stake in the outcome of a dispute. Rhetorical questions demand

engagement. They are as close to an actual conversation with jurors as you can get. You'll frame questions for the desired answer, and they'll answer them. They are extremely effective, whether asked alone or in combinations, one after another. Rhetorical questions are also effective in forcing unscripted physical reactions from jurors – head nods, smiles, raised eyebrows. You will use these to adjusting your argument on the fly based on what you're seeing.

2. ***Metaphors*** are a form of judgmental heuristic that we all use daily. They are among the most common of mental shortcuts and, in a time-constrained setting like closing arguments, they can make powerful points quickly. You'll use them to rest your message on top of a foundation of beliefs and heuristics your jurors accepted long ago.

Let's get started.

Passion

The Takeaway:

- ***Infuse your closing argument with a deep passion. Research shows a message presented passionately has a sharply-increased chance of acceptance regardless of content. Passion is a judgmental heuristic hard-wired into our brains.***
- ***People of every culture heavily rely on a speaker's passion as a major tool for deciding whether to believe and accept the message.***
- ***Passionate closings are vastly more likely to result in favorable verdicts than dispassionate, intellectual closings.***

Passion, the "P" in PERM, as I use the concept in this book, is the presentation of your arguments as a forceful, emotional appeal. You must build powerful emotional appeal into your closing argument. In this context, the emotional force of your argument does not need to have, and will usually not have, any specific bearing on the issue being discussed. In other words, the use of emotional force in your closing argument is not dependent on a logical connection between the force of your presentation and a fact or legal issue in the case. It is the concept articulated by the Greek philosopher Aristotle as *pathos* - persuasion accomplished through the force of emotional appeal and persuasion. Knowing this is as important as understanding your case.

This is not to say you should yell, cry or otherwise display inappropriate emotion to the jury. Rather, passion as a successful summation technique involves a demonstration of deep commitment to your words. This is accomplished through the use of all facets of the PERM system - eye contact, metaphors and rhetorical questions. All contribute to the passion the jury must sense.

Imagine how you might talk if something personal and critically important was on the line for you and your family. Put yourself in that frame of reference. Then ask how your presence, and demeanor, might differ from your closing arguments.

Everything makes a difference when it's personal.

The successful use of pathos at trial depends on your ability to speak with the same deep conviction about your client's interests in front of the jury as you would in speaking about your own family's fundamental needs.

I have developed the following list of pointers useful in developing a more passionate style of argument.

Consider the following at trial to incorporate the concept of *pathos* into your winning closing argument technique:

1. Keep in mind that the goal here is to develop an emotional connection to the jury. That is the fundamental question: Are you creating an emotional bond with each juror?
2. Use the juror questionnaires given to you at the start of jury selection to map out a powerful closing argument. Most

lawyers use this form solely to pick the jury. But the questionnaire is also an excellent tool for identifying themes for closing argument. It contains many clues to the life experiences your jurors bring to the box. Who are they? What joys and pains have they experienced and endured that will lead them to agree with you? What life events have they experienced or endured, and what emotional triggers might they have, that will help you choose your metaphors and rhetorical questions? Family? Marriage? A specific career? Do you have caregivers on your jury? If so, you might speak passionately using metaphors of sharing and caring. Do you have rural families that may relate to themes of community, family and traditional values? Urbanites that might relate to arguments of indifference, anonymity, and the hustle and bustle? People in law enforcement that might relate to rules? People with military backgrounds? These are critical clues for crafting a passionate closing argument. Few trial lawyers present closings that dovetail with the themes I saw in the jury questionnaires. When they do, it is quite obvious, because the jury is noticeably more animated as it listens to their arguments. That questionnaire is top-secret intelligence that will allow you to wrap your message in the jury-specific passion-driven argument.

3. Tie your theme to your client and facts. What is it that your client needs from the jury? Why is that need so deeply personal? If you are defending the case, ask, what is it that your client is being accused of? How might you turn that around to show that the accusations are not only wrong but are deeply personal and contrary to your client's or your witness' nature?
4. Be sure the pitch and tone of your voice match the emotion you're trying to convey. Anger as an emotion should be

reflected in the way you speak. Sadness is often conveyed by a lower volume. Optimism or excitement may be conveyed with a more animated presence, a slightly higher volume, or a faster, more excited pace.

5. Be mindful of your posture, the look on your face, and your voice.
6. Use parables, metaphors, and analogies that inherently invoke sympathy and passion. I have often used my parents, for whom I had the deepest respect, to talk to the jury from a perspective of passionate belief. In one recent age-discrimination trial, I began the closing argument this way, while keeping eye contact with my jurors using the techniques I describe later in this book:

    My mother, who passed away a few years at age 91, was a lifelong stay-at-home mom. In her final years, I made a point to tell her often about the deep influence she had on me and how valuable my time with her had been. I could see the warm appreciation in her eyes as I spoke, as if were checking off boxes on her own list of things she wanted her life to have accomplished. Raising good kids was one of them. I'd refer to her as a "stay-at-home philosopher" because of the many wise observations about the life she shared with me. As she faded from us, but while she was still capable of conversation, I shared these thoughts over and again, always kidding that she could have chaired the philosophy department of the world's finest universities. She would smile so warmly. I admit I didn't see her wisdom when I was growing up. Back then I thought her expressions were a bit outlandish. But over time I came to fully appreciate that they were incredibly shrewd observations about how life works. One of her favorite sayings, to emphasize the importance of making use of every moment, was that regardless

> *of age, we are all on our last cruise. I doubt she made that up, but the point made a lasting impression on me.*

I paused and then referred to my 66-year old plaintiff's long tenure at the company, tying that observation to my client's deep investment of her life in the defendant's operations and success. I continued:

> *And she had another expression that fits here. 'Sooner or later, she would say, we must all sit down at the banquet of consequences.' For the Defendant, that day is today.*

One of the jurors, I could see, teared up slightly. That was passion at work. I wasn't yelling or overselling the harm caused to my client. If anything I was underselling it. But I'd seen that some of the jurors were caregivers, and the brand of passion for this trial had to feed into that. This story has a heartwarming passion to it, and yet requires no yelling or exaggerated gestures. Everyone can relate to their own parent and to warm memories from the past. It is rich with passion, with metaphor, and with eye contact. I stood away from the podium as I shared this, to eliminate barriers between the jury and me, and to make the story and environment so much more personal. Familial parables resonate well in closing because there are always parents on my juries. Everyone listens intently. Jurors respond especially well to a lawyer's personal revelations, given the reputation of lawyers as being hard-boiled professionals indifferent to the feelings of others. This is the use of *pathos.*

7. Step away from the podium as court rules permit. Podiums are barriers between you and the jury. They are formal and ritualistic. They discourage passion. Some lawyers hide behind them as a crutch. Familiarize yourself with your

court's rules. Some judges do not permit you to step from behind the podium. Fair enough. You cannot violate the rules. But most courts allow some degree of movement, with the most common restriction being that you cannot get so close to the jury that you are invading their personal space. If you are not leaving the podium entirely, consider stepping to the side and using the podium to rest an elbow, so you still present in a more casual, conversational manner. Coming out from behind the podium is critical. You become vulnerable. The jury will sense that. The absence of barriers facilitates bonding and enhances a sense of *pathos.* This is one reason TV crews zoom in on speakers who are talking about matters of deep importance. Close-in shots remove visual barriers and create a sense of intimacy. That's what stepping away from the podium does for you in a jury setting.

8. If the subject matter does not appeal to you, is dry, or if you are not a particularly animated personality, study and use the techniques taught at the top-ranking film and acting programs in the country. These are often referred to as the Stanislavski or Strasberg systems or method (or sometimes generically as "method acting.") I've studied "the method" informally for years. The technique trains actors to infuse roles with their own life experiences and to play the role by immersing themselves in the circumstances of the character. This forces actors to ask, "What if I were in the same situation as my character? How would I deliver these thoughts?" This immersive technique makes the scene more relatable and more likely to result in a performance the audience will accept as authentic. If you sense your performance is somewhat mechanical, the use of method acting techniques can be effective for maximizing your passion during closing arguments. There are several

excellent books for learning how to use basic method-acting principles to lend your personal authenticity to the stories of your clients. Among them: "Meisner on Acting" by Sanford Meisner; the book series "An Actor Prepares" by Constantin Stanislavski; "Improvisation for the Theater" by Viola Spolin; "Stanislavski in Practice: Exercises for Students" by Nick O'Brien; and "How to Stop Acting" by Harold Guskin.

I realize that recommending a degree of immersion in method acting will strike some as ridiculous. That is fine. This book is not about what everyone already does. It is about what no one does. Lawyers who follow consensus thinking about closing arguments are the targets, not the beneficiaries, of the PERM system. The consensus-driven thought is by definition not original. In contrast, the PERM method is a truly novel approach that systemizes closing arguments using scientifically-sound compliance research. Elements of PERM have long been taught to, and put into use by, experts in other fields, including acting, advertising, and politics. All three fields depend on psychological compliance techniques. But this is a cutting-edge strategy in the context of closing arguments and for lawyers generally. I have long studied and borrowed techniques from other occupations in my trial practice because of their cross-over value. There is considerable research supporting this strategy, meaning the immersion in other fields as a way of generating new and original thought in one's own line of work.

There is a risk in using the PERM system, but not in the way you might expect. The only risk is that it may require you to swim away from others who follow traditional notions of closing arguments, and upon whom you may rely for a living. Hugging the shoreline is a consensus approach; swimming straight out, where the next island can't be seen yet, is not. This is why I devoted tremendous effort to identifying compliance techniques that have been proven by dozens of studies in the last hundred years by experts in psychology. It is the clustering and organization of these principles into a system for closing arguments that is novel. But there is nothing novel about the four elements themselves. You are safe, and you will see a sharp increase in victories at trial as compared to consensus-approach adversaries. This is true even against those with vastly greater experience.

The message matters, but the presentation mechanics matter more. Why? Because the jury is hearing two stories that are the *exact opposite* of each other. Worse, the subject matter is often beyond them. Even basic lawsuits can be beyond the comprehension of the average person. Jurors compensate for the lack of subject-matter expertise by using heuristics, like those in PERM, to decide what to believe. This is why the science of compliance makes you the heavy favorite in any contest against a foe who is not using these principles systematically.

Back to the Stanislavski and Strasberg systems.

Method acting is the gold standard for the art of infusing someone else's story with your own personal passion. Thus it makes no difference that others may laugh at your use of method-acting techniques to develop a more powerful closing-argument skill set. Some of the highest-paid persuaders in our society - actors and actresses - reached superstar status by practicing and using these methods. Borrowing best-of-class techniques from other occupations is a staple for most world-class performers. Method acting has for decades been the most widely-accepted style for professionals whose occupation is the selling of beliefs to others. Acting is in many ways very similar to the art of the trial, certainly when it comes to closing argument.

The following summary from a course used by a theatre company on the Stanislavski system helps illustrate why it is excellent for boosting your persuasion in closing argument. As you read the explanation, imagine the word "actor" replaced with the word "lawyer," and the word "audience" substituted with the word "jury":

> "Central to Stanislavski's System is believing in what you are doing. Only if the actor believes will the audience believe. They are drawn in by the sincerity of what the actor is doing. Basically the whole System is the set of aids by which the actor is helped to believe he is the role he is creating. Despite the fact the whole System is working towards belief, I find it helpful to do some 'belief exercises with students early on, which can prove a number of important things, starting with the realization that belief 'in limbo' is well-nigh impossible."

The theatre company used the following sample exercise, based on the Stanislavski system, to train actors to authentically and passionately present the events of others. The exercise requires actors to take a blank envelope, with a blank sheet of paper inside, and react as if the paper were a letter containing either very good or very bad news. They are given half dozen imaginary scenarios and told to open the envelope and react accordingly. Since the letter and envelope are blank, actors learn to draw on their own prior experiences to authentically portray these fictional accounts. It is a very effective technique for teaching the skill of infused emotion. The scenarios require the actors to imagine the envelope contains, among other things:

- a love letter
- a coded message containing escape plans
- exam results
- a letter calling off the engagement
- news of the death of a rich old aunt from whom you are due to inherit
- the offer of a job
- news that your son has been killed in the war
- the letter has been given to you by mistake - it should really have gone to another member of your family

Each alternative with the envelope requires a different emotion. This compels successful actors to develop an on-demand ability to marry authentic personal emotions to borrowed facts. Not one of these scenarios is personal or real to the acting professional, but you will believe it is. That is why method acting works, and why it works for trial lawyers seeking to gain an edge. You present passion as authentically to juries as you would in your own life. The transformation for me was amazing, as I began to speak to juries in a way that felt deeply personal, even as I was only recounting my client's experiences. The disconnect between my feelings and the client's story vanished. Notes become irrelevant at the point when you can use pathos as a technique. You will not need them. Reading from notes undermines your ability to convey passion. You must break your reliance on notes in order to use the PERM system. Reliance on notes conveys inauthenticity.

Eye Contact

The Takeaway:

- ***You should aim to spend roughly 80-85% of your closing argument looking at the jury, with the balance referring to your most powerful exhibits.***
- ***Psychology researchers have shown that eye contact is a major indicator of a speaker's truthfulness and own belief in the message.***
- ***Use the "Lazy 8" and other techniques described here to sharply increase your ability to maintain eye contact, and to learn the best ways to look at individual jurors.***

Eye contact, the "E" in PERM, is every bit as important as *pathos,* rhetorical questions, and metaphors. Eye contact in Western societies is a fundamental tool of communication. In other societies, that is not always true; it can be an inappropriate sign of intimacy or familiarity. Not so, however, in most Western cultures and particularly in the United States.

Some researchers believe eye contact is so powerful a force because it is connected with humans' earliest survival patterns. Children who could attract and maintain eye contact, and therefore increase attention, had the best chance of being fed and cared for. Today, newborns instinctively lock eyes with their caregivers. And the power of that infantile eye contact still retains its impact on the adult mind. Whether it's shifty-eyed guilt or wide-eyed innocence, we automatically assign enormous credence to the signals we give and get when we look each other in the eyes. (Google "eye gazing parties" to read about a novel form of entertainment that relies exclusively on eye contact, without words, as a form of communication.)

So the expression that the eyes are the windows to the soul, while clichéd, is accurate. There are few better mechanisms for judging another's truthfulness and commitment than by watching the eyes, and jurors heavily rely on eye contact to accept one message over another. Indeed, our system of justice revolves around eye contact and demeanor. We construct special rooms (courtrooms) where people with information (witnesses) must sit in special chairs and directly face those who must judge their truthfulness. The trial phase – the phase where freedom may be lost, where financial ruin may result, and where lives can be changed forever – takes place in a setting created at astounding expense to ensure eye contact between those who judge and those who are to be judged. Think about that for a moment. Isn't that amazing? No one really stops to ponder the chief reason we have courtrooms, but it's eye contact. It's to have a place where those charged with deciding the outcome of important disputes can look directly at the interested parties. Imagine the money that could be saved if judges or juries could simply read testimony or even just listen to recordings of it, and also looking online at scanned copies of the exhibits. This could be done easily. It's already done this way for lesser legal proceedings such as contested unemployment compensation hearings in some states. In those jurisdictions, hearing officers take all testimony by phone and read the exhibits submitted by the parties. They make a decision without ever seeing the witnesses. But it's not done this way for society's larger disputes. That we go to such lengths and expense to construct courthouses and courtrooms says a great deal about the extraordinary value of eye contact and demeanor.

And, just as making eye contact sends a powerful message, so does avoiding it. Those charged with finding the truth in every setting imaginable – juries, law enforcement officers, and military interrogators, of course, but also parents, spouses, teachers, and salespeople – draw sharp conclusions from the avoidance of eye contact. Such evasion, often referred to as gaze avoidance, cutoff or "eye blocking," is seen as an effort to avoid revealing through eye contact what one is not saying verbally. Some studies even associate prolonged gaze avoidance with psychopathy and other mental disorders. This says a great deal about the impact eye contact has, positive or negative. Think about how you have used eye gaze (or avoidance) as a factor in dating, marriage, and business transactions. The chances are that you will react negatively in any setting where the person will not look at you.

Yet many lawyers I have opposed in courtrooms relied heavily on notes during the closing argument. It appeared to be a crutch, or perhaps a safe place similar to the podium. Imagine going on a date and sitting across the table and talking about your likes and dislikes as you read from a sticky note. Or, imagine sitting in a job interview and talking about career likes and dislikes while scrolling though notes on your tablet or smartphone. Will you get a second date, or a job offer? If you think reliance on notes in these settings sends the wrong message, what might jurors think about your inability to look at them and talk from the heart?

The sheer volume of psychological research on eye contact is noteworthy. Some findings I discovered during my analysis of the major studies on this topic are useful in judging how much eye contact to maintain with your juries:

- The proper amount of eye contact – that which produces a feeling of likability and trustworthiness – varies with situations, settings, personality types, gender and cultural differences. As a general rule, normative direct eye contact ranges from 50% to 60% of the time during an ordinary social conversation. The higher the percentage of eye contact, research shows, the more credible you will be considered. In other words, the odds your message will be accepted rises in tandem with eye contact. Research also shows that the more critical the topic, the more we expect heavy eye contact. Such contact in our most life-changing conversations, for example, may rise to 100%. In a jury setting, this means jurors' acceptance of your message may depend on your ability to maximize eye contact.
- • Eye contact produces a powerful, subconscious sense of connection that extends even to drawn or photographed eyes, a fact demonstrated by researchers at Cornell University. They manipulated the gaze of the cartoon rabbit on several Trix cereal boxes, and then asked a panel of adults to choose one. They discovered, as expected, that the box most frequently chosen was the one on which the rabbit was looking directly at them, rather than away.
- Scientific research shows that we reduce eye contact when we are talking about something shameful or embarrassing, when we are sad or depressed, and when we are accessing internal thoughts or emotions. We increase eye contact when dealing with people we like, admire, or who have power over us. In more intense or intimate conversations,

we naturally look at each another more often, and hold that gaze for longer periods of time. In fact, we judge relationships by the amount of eye contact exchanged: the greater the eye contact, the closer the relationship. What might this mean for trial lawyers? You should look directly at jurors when discussing weaknesses in your case. Looking down at your notes when you deny an accusation is likely to signal deceptive gaze avoidance. Make your denials firm and bold. You must look at the jurors when denying key accusations. Watch your adversary in closing carefully in your next trial, and informally note how often the lawyer looks down when denying a matter. Those whose career misfortunes include being unaware of this heuristic or rule of thumb relating to the avoidance of eye contact when denying accusations will do so instinctively at a very high rate. The jury will notice, too.

- Females look more at those with whom they are talking than males. For this reason, academic research has shown, women are more likely to prefer a face-to-face conversation, while men are content to talk standing side-by-side. In your trials, the research suggests, eye contact may rise in importance as a PERM element, and even become a critical ally, when a significant percentage of your jurors are female.
- As a corollary to the previous principles, studies show a speaker who actively seeks out eye contact is judged to be more believable, confident and competent.

I saw an example of the impact eye contact can have on the outcome of a trial one evening while writing this book. I was watching an old episode of Dateline NBC that featured a segment about a husband accused of killing his spouse. At trial and in one particularly critical moment of the prosecutor's closing arguments, the prosecutor was reading his argument from notes in his hand. As he reached an especially powerful moment in his argument....he completely lost his place on the page. It was not clear what caused this, but the fact that he did was painfully obvious, as there was a terribly awkward pause as he tried to figure out where he'd left off. Even I felt very uncomfortable, despite the fact that I was sitting in my living room and watching an old video of a trial from a few years past. I had the feeling, just as the research shows, that his inability to speak from the heart was a sign that he did not believe what he was saying.

This was not an act of dishonesty or intentional eye blocking. But it underscored the point. The prosecutor wasn't speaking from the heart. He was reading a script. And when he lost his place, like a Broadway actor who breaks character for help with the line, his authenticity vaporized. He was an actor. It was a script. And he lost. The husband was acquitted and is a free man.

In fairness, I doubt this moment alone determined the outcome, but it probably had a role. It suggested the prosecutor did not have a heartfelt belief in his own words because he had to read them to the jury. This awkward moment said something powerful, and unfortunate. When he lost his place, he could not look up and share his heartfelt feelings, because he had none. That may have tipped the balance in favor of the defendant because the jury, faced with conflicting evidence, likely chose the side that most appeared to believe their own story.

And don't we do that ourselves? Aren't we more likely to believe someone else when we are satisfied they also believe what they're saying?

How insincere do we seem to juries when we read our own "scripts" and don't maintain eye contact?

It may seem harsh to equate the absence of steady eye contact, by reading from notes, with insincerity, but it is true. We never need notes to talk about matters of deep truth. We look directly at the person with whom we are speaking and open up. I mentioned job interviews and dating already. But there are many others. Imagine tucking your daughter into bed, gently kissing her forehead, and then retrieving a list of bullet points and reading the words "Sleep tight! I love you!" Most parents would consider this an act to be high treason. And how might this seem to your child? What parent doesn't maintain steady eye contact during important conversations with their children? We don't use notes in those settings because our feelings and beliefs are authentic. In that setting, notes are irrelevant, and they are irrelevant because we believe what we say. Your daughter or son would probably start crying if you pulled out a checklist and said you loved them. We never use or need notes when we speak from the heart. Our children and spouses understand that. So do juries.

PERM requires you to put your notes down and look at the jury. It's fine to have a small note sheet with a few bullet points to work from, but they should be true bullet points, not a full outline. I recommend no more than two or three words per point. Think "abbreviated headline." If you can speak passionately, and believe what you are saying, you don't need lengthy notes.

The PERM method requires you to break the notes addiction. Your credibility will rise sharply, particularly in comparison to adversaries who read their notes. The visual difference to a jury is striking.

How to break this habit? There are several ways to do it, and you can begin in modest settings. You'll soon see that the sensation of speaking note-free is surprisingly liberating. Your own personal authenticity will skyrocket.

Try it first at low-risk court hearings. It could be an uncontested hearing on a motion to amend a pleading, or something similar, where there is nothing in controversy and nothing to lose from a rough start to your note-less trial career. I use a sticky note to hold my bullet points because it is easy to reference and will not appear to anyone as a script. Moreover, and because the size of a sticky note limits what you can write, it forces you to synthesize your arguments. If your bullet points do not fit on a two-inch-square sticky note, you have too many.

You can transition over several weeks to lengthier presentations at mediations or more substantive, contested hearings. My first major test of an entirely note-free presentation, years ago, was at a summary judgment hearing. It went well in part because I had worked up to that stage. I then began going note-free in all my proceedings. I do always use bullet points because I am not about to miss a major argument just for the sake of being note-free. That could be malpractice. But I aggressively minimize them because I need that precious eye contact with the jury. As a result, I spend virtually the entire time speaking from the heart and looking at the jury.

I should mention that I frequently make eye contact with jurors during direct and cross examinations, not just closing arguments. It is a subtler, casual glance. I will occasionally look at the jury, but only momentarily, as if I were also talking to them and to involve them in the discussion. This is a technique I use to further engage them as active participants in the trial. I never look at the jury to ask the entire question, of course. Prolonged contact like that in the midst of examination is improper. But casual contact is not only proper but essential to your overall presentation.

Specifically, I will sometimes step away from the podium to emphasize a point to the witness on the stand, and turn slightly and briefly to look at the jury as I ask the question. This is an effective technique in quickly assessing the jury's level of engagement and agreement with my examination topics. Then I turn back to the podium and continue the examination. It is something I regularly do. To illustrate, I may during an hour-long examination look directly at jurors five to ten times, depending. That's a range of six to twelve minutes between instances of eye contact. Why? Because I want to constantly engage the jury, but it's not a staring contest. It's not "Get a load of this!" It's more subtle – a way of saying, "I respect your role."

This technique is also a useful gauge to judge juror reactions to a particular piece of evidence or testimony. If the jury looks indifferent, bored, or in disagreement with me, I will see that and adjust accordingly. So eye contact is a regulatory tool, and important for making incremental modifications in your presentation. You are missing valuable feedback if you are not checking in with your jury during any examination in the jury's presence. Know your jury. The way to know them is to engage them throughout the trial. There is a great deal of valuable intelligence emanating from the jury box at all times.

Now, if the thought of regularly looking at the jury makes you squeamish, I would encourage you to start modestly, and ramp up slowly on your journey to a note-free closing argument. Once you see just how far you can go with this, and how effective it is, you'll never go back. There is nothing wrong with it. I have never had an objection from an opposing lawyer or a judge to my eye contact with the jury. Juries are a critical element of every trial, and deserve to be involved and acknowledged at every step. The best trial lawyers in our country do everything but take a seat in the jury box. You may be surprised at the extent to which you can engage the jury this way. You will own them.

Of course, you should not ask questions that are inappropriate just to get a reaction from the jury, and you should not ask questions of a witness that have only nominal relevance to the outcome and are simply intended to tilt the jury in your favor. That will draw objections and may have the opposite effect regarding the jury's view of you.

Make Your Exhibits Your Talking Points

Another technique I always use for powerful summations without notes is to use admitted exhibits to review the evidence. If there is a particularly important report, letter or another document that captures the essence of a specific point, display that on the courtroom projector and talk about it. If you need to have paper in front of you, this is an outstanding way to do it. Using admitted evidence allows you to score key points during closing without a single note.

This is the same trick used by professional speakers who rely on slide presentations. They work from the bullet points on the slides, to avoid the need to use notes at any point during their speech. In a real way, their slides are their notes. But no one thinks of it that way.

So the exhibits will be your slides. And they'll allow you to argue by discussing their contents, which you'll already know by heart. This trick provides the best of all worlds. The document is, in a crude sort of way, a script. But it won't strike the jury that way. You didn't write it, and you didn't organize it. You're just pointing out its critical provisions. Using documents or exhibits in your closing is a very effective way to break the habit of lengthy notes. I will quickly grab a set of 10 or 15 key documents, stack them up and walk to the podium. Then I work through the documents in whatever order I think makes sense. I can still use a small sticky note with my bullet points, again consisting of just one or two words, but the majority of my presentation will remain note free.

You can choose the desired set of exhibits for this purpose well before the start of the trial. You should be able to identify the key documents for and against you. Make a set of those before the trial starts, so you have them separate and ready to go when closing arguments began. If you can't do that, then assemble your "talking points exhibits" during a break in the trial to pick them out from the set of admitted exhibits. It's usually fine to show the jury a photocopy of an admitted exhibit rather than the actual exhibit itself. In other words, if time is short and you cannot pick through a large number of admitted exhibits before closing begins, use a duplicate photocopy of the admitted exhibits that you preselected before or during trial. I've never had anyone complain about that. Failing this, have someone retrieve the actual exhibits by number, using the list compiled before trial of the exhibits you would want to mention during closing.

Maintain regular, steady eye contact with the jury as you discuss each exhibit. Enlarge or reduce the exhibit on the overhead projector as necessary, always turning to the jury to discuss the key points of the document. Explain what it is, what it says and why it's important. This technique allows for heavy eye contact with the jury. It works exceedingly well because it allows you to focus on critical evidence and to talk from the heart because you will already be familiar with the contents of those documents.

How should you make your eye contact? I recommend a lazy horizontal figure-eight eye gaze (the "Lazy 8"). In other words, (a) start at the back-row-far-left juror, (b) work slowly downward and across toward the front-row-far-right juror, and then (c) move up visually and make eye contact with the back-row-far-right juror and follow the same pattern, down and across, to the front-row-far-left juror. The lazy-eight pattern is used by many professional presenters because it appears random and does not strike close-range audiences as offensive or intrusive.

Other techniques are fine but not as effective. For example, you could look at jurors one row at a time from left to right, but this has a more mechanical appearance. The magic of the lazy-eight approach is that as you crisscross from top left to bottom right and again from top right to bottom left, it will appear that you are engaging many of the jurors at one time. It is a more relaxed and natural technique. Another problem with scanning one row at a time is that it will likely appear that you are ignoring the entirety of the other rows. The lazy-eight technique blends your gaze across multiple rows as you speak.

Be mindful, as well, of what you are saying and how it may strike specific jurors. For example, you may inadvertently appear insensitive if, in a disability discrimination case, for example, you gaze directly at the one disabled juror. It may appear you are pandering to that juror if you represent the disabled plaintiff, or that you are bearing down on the disabled juror in an unpleasant way if you are representing the defendant. The same is true of other jurors who may perceive your comments as directed at them. In a recent national-origin employment discrimination trial, in which I represented a Hispanic plaintiff, I visually engaged the one Hispanic juror but in a respectful way consistent with the time spent engaging other jurors. I appreciated his service on the jury but did not want to convey the impression I was trying to exploit his national origin.

Remember what I said about tucking your little one into bed and pulling out a 3 x 5 card and reading the words "I love you." That would be outrageous, wouldn't it? You would never do that, and you would never need to because you know what you feel and there is no script needed. The concept is exactly the same in front of juries. If you are reading from a script, you are selling insincerity. You are an actor who failed to memorize his or her lines or to buy into them at such a level that you can speak from the heart without reading them.

The Memory Palace Technique

One last tip. Another tremendously helpful way to avoid the need for notes is to improve your memorization skills. The average person has the capacity to memorize tremendous quantities of information, but never even comes close to doing so.

I began using Memory Palace techniques when I was a teenager, and they've served me well during my career as a lawyer. I taught it to both of my children, and they developed spectacular memories. One has a successful career in the U.S. Navy and rose swiftly through the ranks in part because of her memorization skills. The other is at an elite university in the Northeast, and his ability to memorize test material in high school helped get him there. If you're not familiar with the concept of a Memory Palace, I recommend two resources. One is a short video on YouTube by Ron White, from the National Geographic show Brain

Games. Search for "Mind Palace Technique, " and it should pop up among the top results. That video is just six minutes long, so it won't take long, and it's among the best introductions. Another resource is a book called Moonwalking with Einstein, by Joshua Foer. That book is about his journey toward entry in the United States Memory Championships. It's also an excellent introduction to the Memory Palace technique for developing world-class memorization skills.

Memory Palace training goes far beyond the scope of this book. I mention it here only because it is another outstanding presentation mechanics tool. Suffice it to say for now that the Memory Palace technique uses visualization to store, organize and retrieve information. By example, as my kids got older, we would have contests to see who could memorize the most license tags of passing vehicles on the highway. Our family best was something in the range of 25 cars. The tricks of the memory Palace are thousands of years old and have been used widely by memory experts to store prodigious amounts of information. Memory Athletes (MAs) who compete in the US Memory Championships can store amazing amounts of information in a very short period and compete to see who can recall the most detail. Most use the Memory Palace technique, with some occasional variation. Some examples of the competitions there:

- **The Names and Faces Competition** allows MAs "...15 minutes to memorize 117 color photos of different people (head and shoulder shots) with a first and second name written below each picture. Once the memorization period is over, competitors are then given 20 minutes for recall. Mental athletes are given the same photos again but without the names and in a different order to that on the memorization sheet. A point is awarded for every correctly spelled name, either first or last. No points are awarded for phonetic spellings.

- **Spoken Words Event.** Here Mental Athletes (MAs) will have 15 minutes to memorize a list of 200 words organized numerically in five columns with 20 words per column (2 pages). MAs must start at the first word of column 1 and remember as many of the words as possible. The word list is comprised of concrete nouns, abstract nouns, and verbs. Once the memorization period is over, the MAs will be randomly ordered to begin the oral recall of words. Recall will begin with the first word in the first column and continue consecutively. Each MA will be allowed up to 15 seconds to answer. The first 3 MAs who either identify the incorrect word or fail to recall a word are immediately eliminated.

In other words, the competitors successfully learn, organize and store enormous amounts of random information in extremely short periods of time. These competitions take place both in the United States and worldwide. The amount of information that has to be learned by even novice MAs dwarfs anything that a lawyer must present during a closing argument. That's why the technique is very effective for lawyers. The Memory Palace techniques would easily allow you to make the transition to a note-free presentation.

Rhetorical Questions

The Takeaway:

- ***Psychological research shows rhetorical questions are devastatingly effective in engaging and persuading audiences that themselves have no direct, personal stake in the outcome of a dispute.***
- ***There are four or five different ways to structure your use of them, each very effective. Mix up your tactics for maximum impact.***

R**hetorical questions** are an equally powerful tool of persuasion that the majority of lawyers overlook. The research confirms that rhetorical questions are an incredible tool for persuading passive audiences (i.e., those that cannot speak with freedom equal to that of the speaker) because they involve the recipient in the message and heighten the sense of personal relevance. They also increase "message processing," meaning the level of brain activity in evaluating the answer suggested by the question.

Here's something else to think about that has particular relevance to trial lawyers. There is a substantial body of evidence that persuading people requires different approaches depending on whether the audience considers the matter at hand to be personally important to them. Listeners who consider the topic to be of genuine personal significance are more likely to actively engage with the content itself. Personally-affected audiences are more concerned about a correct outcome, so they devote more attention to reaching the proper outcome. Conversely, people who see a matter as having little or no personal relevance are more likely to use superficial criteria, such as perceived social pressures or even the attractiveness of the speaker. Since they are not personally affected by a bad outcome, they are less invested and apt to consider shallow/nonsensical factors that could result in the wrong decision. But research has shown that the use of rhetorical questions changes the way low-involvement audiences process the information and tend to better motivate such audiences to engage in the message. A juror who is not naturally inclined to process your message is more likely to do so if you include rhetorical questions in your message presentation toolkit.

This is a finding of great significance to trial lawyers. Juries are often called to decide on cases that will have no lasting personal effect on them. That makes the use of devices that draw in and engage the jurors all the more important. Rhetorical questions are proven to do exactly that. Lawyers that fail to use rhetorical questions as a device in their arsenal are missing a critical opportunity. Again, there is considerable literature in the scientific community to suggest that frivolous considerations such as who has the more attractive lawyer can indeed affect the verdict. If I found myself in trial against a former supermodel who went to law school, it would behoove me to ensure the jury is actively engaged on an intellectual level by increasing my use of rhetorical questions. That would allow me to steer the jury toward consideration of the real issues.

Rhetorical questions, of course, are not expected to elicit an audible answer. Rather, they are tools in which to make strong positive or negative assertions in the form of an interrogative. How you word them affects their meaning as well as the likely answer triggered in the minds of your jurors.

University of Pennsylvania researcher Chung-Hye Han offers the following examples of similarly-worded rhetorical questions to illustrate how slight changes in phrasing lead to opposite answers, something to be mindful of in formulating your questions.

Consider the following two rhetorical questions:

(a) Did I tell you that writing a dissertation was easy?
(b) Didn't I tell you that writing a dissertation was easy?

These questions respectively assert, "I didn't tell you that writing a dissertation was easy" in example (a), and "I told you that writing a dissertation was easy" in example (b). These illustrate a key feature of rhetorical questions, which is that the desired response to the question is usually the exact opposite of what was asked. This essential quality is sometimes referred to as "negative polarity." In other words, the positive "did" and negative "didn't" in these yes-no questions are framed to elicit the opposite answer. The "did" question implies "did not" and the "did not" questions implies the answer "did." Both are bold declarative statements, not questions.

So take pains to ensure your questions, however phrased, trigger the mental response you intend.

Some tips for effective rhetorical questions:

1. Frame the question so the answer is as short as possible. A one-word mental response from the jury is ideal. "Did

Mr. Williams bother to read the contract?" is more effective than "What reasons did Mr. Williams have to sign it without reading?" With some exceptions I'll talk about in a moment, rhetorical questions are not effective in closing argument if the answer requires extended thought for the jury. You will be moving on to your next point while they are still trying to suss out the multi-pronged answers to the last question. You will lose the jury that way. Take pains to ensure that your questions call for a simple yes or no most of the time. That is far and away the most effective type of rhetorical question in a summation setting. If a very short answer is enough to be informative, keep it that way.

2. If you do have a legitimate multi-point answer to the rhetorical question you posed, immediately move into the points you wish to make, so the jury is not left behind pondering your question. For example, you might introduce a related set of facts with a question like, "Just how hard did Sally Davis work to resolve this before coming in this courtroom?", and then answer your own question with, "Let's take a look at the evidence" and move quickly into the points. Keep the number of points to five or less and make each swift and powerful. Remember you must hit home runs. Do not use this technique to rehash the evidence.
3. It is fine to use multiple rhetorical questions in a row, but do so sparingly to avoid wearing the jury out. "Why would Mr. Williams waste one second of his time going back to her apartment? Why would he lie about that? Wouldn't her own family support his version of events only if it were absolutely true?" A series of questions like this can powerfully engage the jury. The use of serial rhetorical questions is excellent for throwing knockout punches with your evidence because it has an almost headline-like attention-getting impact in a quiet courtroom. It is very dramatic. But it is unwise to ask more than four or five in a row, because the high

engagement triggered by rhetorical questions can drain the mental gas tank of your jury.

4. Still another potent approach is to ask sequential rhetorical questions but, this time, insert short, punchy answers in between them. This tactic will have you asking the question and answering them, one after another. For example, in a car accident case, the injured victim's lawyer might ask rhetorically, *"What did Ms. Williams do after slamming into Christopher Edwards? NOTHING. What did Mr. Edwards do? NOTHING. When did they report it? NEVER. What did they do next? WENT HOME AND SLEPT LIKE BABIES."* This style can have an almost nuclear-bomb style impact in a courtroom. It is fantastic when used to stir up the jury's emotion about particularly callous conduct. A question like this might be asked with grave pathos, with direct eye contact, and then answered with great force aloud, or alternating forceful questions with soft answers, to contrast the callous conduct of the wrongdoers (loud) with the impact on the innocent victims (soft).
5. An equally-commanding tactic, which can be used in conjunction with and to follow the prior one (question-answer-question-answer in a fast, forceful style), is to then ask two or three rhetorical questions without answers, e.g., *Why? Why?* To pick up on the prior example, a personal-injury lawyer might say, "you heard that Ms. Williams did absolutely nothing to help Christopher Edwards after she struck him and saw him lying there, dying. *Why? Why?* The pace, tone and visible pathos is key to delivery, but the effect is overwhelming.
6. Use them to attack gaps in the adversary's evidence, e.g., *Where are the documents? Where is the CEO? Where are the witnesses to support anything the company said in opening statements? Why would the company make those claims and then fail to support any of them? Why?*

7. Use them to cast doubt on the credibility of the adversary's evidence. *Does anything they said about that make any sense whatsoever? Is night day, and day night?*
8. Use them to frame your client with positive qualities. *Who went out of their way to qualify for the position? To interview? Who worked day and night, seven days a week for the next year to turn the department around? Who took online classes, who published guides, and, taught others?*
9. Use them with metaphors - an excellent technique to further engage the jury. *Why would she take that journey, down into the valley, alone, unless she were completely committed to the company? Why would she leave her husband and her children back at base camp, unless she were completely committed to the company?* As mentioned earlier, the PERM elements can all be used in combination, all at once, even in a single sentence. These two questions, for example, could be directed to the jury with great passion and with direct eye contact. A well-framed rhetorical question, presented with deep personal passion, a metaphor and direct eye contact can deal a devastating blow to the adversary and literally *silence* the entire courtroom.

As these examples illustrate, and as a century of academic and psychological research proves, rhetorical questions can deliver victory like no other linguistic technique. You will see a material increase in wins at trial using them. I think some lawyers are afraid to ask questions in front of the jury this way, perhaps feeling that doing so makes them look presumptuous or theatrical in a circus-ringmaster kind of way. Put that out of your mind. There is enormous force and power behind the asking of rhetorical questions. The asking of questions forces the listener to answer them silently. It forces your jury to become mentally engaged. But they are also an effective device for presenting persuasive argument when varied in style as I have discussed, including (a) a single question alone,

(b) multiple questions without answers, (c) multiple questions punctuated by short, powerful answers and (d) short questions without answers. The pathos evident in your style will also be an important element, as will eye contact.

I recall from seeing many of Martin Luther King's recorded speeches that his use of rhetorical questions was so powerful that the audiences would literally shout out answers, over and over. Here's an excerpt from a speech he gave in 1965 that mixed all the elements of the PERM system and more. It beautifully illustrates the power of such questions, particularly when mixed with metaphors, pathos and eye contact. There is nothing more effective:

> I know you are asking today, "How long will it take?" Somebody's asking, "How long will prejudice blind divisions of men, darken their understanding, and drive bright-eyed wisdom from her sacred throne?' Somebody's asking, "When will wounded justice, lying prostrate on the streets of Selma and Birmingham and communities all over the South, be lifted from this dust of shame to reign supreme among the children of men??' Somebody's asking, "When will the radiant star of hope be plunged against the nocturnal bosom of this lonely nights, plucked from weary souls with chains of fear and the manacles of death? How long will justice be crucified, and truth bear it?

Audiences attending his speeches reacted that way, with unbridled passion, anger, joy and power, because they could. Rhetorical questions literally beg the audience to talk back, to engage with you, to get into the game. There is a limit to a jury's display of engagement, of course. But you will stir the same level of engagement and emotion.

METAPHORS

The Takeaway:

- ***Metaphors are a fast, time-efficient way to sell ideas because they build on existing beliefs and perceptions (compared to pitching ideas without utilizing your jurors' existing thoughts).***
- ***Incorporate metaphors freely during your closing. They are less taxing mentally than rhetorical questions, so there is little risk of overuse.***
- ***Use the jurors' interests and life experiences, laid out for the taking in the juror questionnaires and possibly further developed during trial using social media profiles, to choose the source domains (explained later) for your metaphors. This information will tell you figuratively, the "language" your jurors speak, and that you need to speak to them.***

Metaphors, the "M" in the PERM system, have been studied extensively in the field of psychology. The reason is that the scientific research has shown that information presented through the use of metaphors is processed unusually fast by the brain. Great effort has been expended to understand why. One theory is that because metaphors link new information being presented to information we already know and understand, mental processing requires less effort. A good metaphor matches the new with the old by bridging common concepts between them. Put another way, metaphors work because they are property-matching devices. One invokes the image of the other, and we draw a mental conclusion that the two are similar. This method of simply adding new knowledge to an existing base requires less learning, theorists posit, and so people "get it" much faster.

That is exactly what makes them perfect for closing arguments.

A good metaphor will link flattering (or unflattering) properties to the thing you are discussing in a faster, more compact and more memorable way than you can with literal argument.

The psychology behind metaphors is complex, and there are more than a dozen different styles of metaphor. There is no need to discuss the scientific literature on each of the variants because this is not an academic work. This is a practical guide to constructing powerful closing arguments. It is sufficient for the scope of this book to say there is a heavy body of scientific research showing that metaphors are highly effective in gaining compliance from an audience. In other words, they are effective in persuading the audience to buy what you are selling and to believe what you are saying.

For purposes of helping you consistently create good metaphors, let's walk through the basics. A good metaphor has three parts: the **tenor**, the **vehicle**, and the **ground.**

The tenor is the *subject* of the metaphor.

The vehicle is the thing to which your subject is compared.

The ground is the characteristic the two have in common.

The goal is to get your jurors to see the similarity, or common ground, between the two.

Imagine two young troublemaking children who see their father pull up into the driveway. One says "*Here comes the Terminator.*" In just four words the child created an outstanding metaphor. No deep thought required. Got it.

In this example, the tenor – the subject - is the dad, the vehicle is the Terminator, and the ground (linking subject and vehicle), or comparable qualities are "aggressive," "cold, and "assailant."

A good metaphor uses an instantly-recognizable <u>vehicle</u> – something all jurors will instantly understand as having the positive or negative qualities you are going to paint your target with. It could be your client, a witness, a document, a key decision or an outcome. It's that simple.

This is all you need to be a metaphor architect of the highest order. Think of the qualities you want the jury to associate with the subject of your argument. Then think of something well-known to everyone and that people associate with the desired positive or negative qualities. Then come up with the statement that links the two. For example, is a particular workplace a public servant's paradise? Or an ethical swamp? You can easily see how your choice of the vehicle determines what qualities you are conveying to the jury. I don't have to explain the concept of paradise, nor of a swamp. That's why metaphors are so powerful for closing argument. They allow you to cover enormous ground very swiftly. If you represent an employee in a workplace-related lawsuit, you could describe your client as "a saint in a sewer." That would likely evoke mental images of someone with a halo canoeing through an awful mess. If you're trying to show that someone's life, or career, was a series of ups and downs, what vehicle or thing would you use to deliver the message? You might say their career was like a yo-yo - up, down, up, down.

The point is that metaphorical references allow you to favorably frame the evidence using linguistic shortcuts. The alternative is to use your closing argument to work through the entire body of evidence, document by document or witness by witness, all over again. That is a colossal waste of time, and it is nominally persuasive compared to true argument.

Metaphors are superior persuasion devices because they rely on associations already deeply ingrained in the audiences' mind. A good metaphor conveys in a few words what would otherwise require lengthy or complicated discussion. You don't have the luxury of time. Nor does the jury. Many jurors, regardless of the duration of your trial, want nothing more than to go home. Metaphors relieve this time crunch because they are time-effective – ten gallons of persuasion in a five-gallon jug.

Many trial lawyers make the mistake of using closing argument to review the evidence at length. That is a poor use of your precious supply of minutes. Your closing should be a powerful statement about the <u>meaning</u> of the evidence. Metaphors are up for the challenge. They allow you to move quickly from one topic to another, and the jury will understand every bit of it.

To illustrate, in a stock-fraud case involving sleazy broker tactics, you could review all the evidence and provide a detailed overview of brokerage-firm operations. In other words, you could try the case all over again in your closing. Or you could use a metaphor, and tell the jury that you just took them on a ride through the sewer in a glass-bottom boat. Which of those two punches harder? Which takes three seconds, and which takes most of your closing argument to make the same point? A literal description of the evidence all over again will annoy the jury. They don't need it. Experienced trial lawyers get right to the point, and their arguments are lively, entertaining, sometimes heartwarming and sometimes gut-wrenching, but always riveting. And they rely heavily on metaphors. It's home run after home run after home run.

In choosing or constructing your own metaphors, it is important to carefully select the qualities you want the jury to associate with your subject. In the example I used of the Terminator above, the quality the two children associated with their dad was something that was very definitely not human and put on this earth to cause pain. There might well be qualities associated with the Terminator that do not serve this purpose, but uncaring and evil are the characteristics most people associate with the character. So it's safe to use if the point is portraying the father unfavorably.

Be certain the vehicle you choose has the qualities that serve your objective. If, in the end, the Terminator were mostly known as a character that crossed over to the good side, a metaphor that described an opposing witness as the Terminator might backfire.

Some vehicles have multiple qualities. Many will simply be irrelevant, so it's not necessary that the vehicle has one and only one quality. It's just important that you be aware of the <u>most likely</u> qualities your jury will see in the vehicle and associate with your subject or tenor. Keep in mind that in most situations your jurors will identify the common ground between your subject and the vehicle without thought. That's the point of the metaphor - to allow the jury to use mental shortcuts. So choose wisely. Some vetting process with your trial team or office staff is useful.

One approach I've used is to gather staff in a conference room and give them each a notepad or sticky notes. I tell them I'm going to mention something and I want them to immediately write down the first word that comes to mind when they hear the thing I've mentioned. I explained that no one is to look at anyone else's notes. Once they write the word down, they must turn the sheet of paper over, and I collect them. This way, there is no reflection or conferral between them. The faster they write down the first thought that comes to mind, the more comfortable I am that my instincts about the qualities the jury will associate with the vehicle are correct. I also have them write down the first word that comes to mind because I want to avoid problems created by what some call "social proof." Research shows that in group settings, many in the group will simply agree with the first opinion expressed out loud, or whatever opinion is expressed by the most senior person in the room. That's because people tend to avoid conflicts and don't want to stir up trouble with opinions that have already been expressed. So they tend to agree with whatever was mentioned first, whether they agree with that or not. That's why I don't allow verbal responses.

This is an excellent technique for test-driving your vehicle. (See how easy metaphors can come to mind?) The faster your staff calls out the first word that comes to mind, the more reliable the result. The key is to discourage excessive thought. We want deeply-rooted associations, and those will surface when the exercise is done at high speed to thwart well-meaning but misguided efforts to guess at what you want to hear.

Metaphors are used in every field and profession. A detailed study of the use of metaphors by politicians was conducted by

Jonathan Chartaris-Black. He found that most of the great speakers tended to work from the same "source domains" – categories – for their metaphor vehicles. These included such categories as journeys ("There are forks in the road, where the path we take determines the future lives of millions of people"), conflicts ("So this is a battle for values, but let's not have that battle amongst ourselves"), light and darkness (e.g., "a lighted path created to help," "the light in her eyes," a "career darkened by injustice"), landscapes ("a jungle of regulation," "valleys of despair"), sleep ("e.g., the "American dream," "allowing our dreams to come true" and "rudely awakened by an insistent alarm bell, slowly rising to her feet, rubbing her eyes and prepared to speak"), health (a "paralysis of decision-making," discrimination as a "tragic cancer within the body of our society"), music ("hit a high note," "struck a chord," "sang their praises," "sang a different tune") buildings (such as references to creating walls between people, or opening doors), the weather (a "climate of fear," and "being left out in the cold"), animals ("we're a different and unique breed," "scratching and clawing their way to the top"), plants (" by the fruits of our labors"), fire (" it sparked our hopes, and fired our imaginations"), destruction ("shattered illusions"), light ("They tried to hide in the shadows, but we shined the light of justice on them"), books (" and that is just the first chapter"), vehicles (" pedaling as fast as she could," "going in reverse") and directions or direction-finding devices ("everything went south," "a roadmap to success," "headed in the wrong direction, "moral compass").

Among the top categories or source domains are the following, with simple starter examples for each:

Journeys (on the trail, down the path, fork in the road)
Destruction (torn down, destroyed, set ablaze)
Human Body (he was her eyes and ears; lent a hand, don't set foot)

Plants (blossomed, died on the vine, picking the petals off)
Conflict (fighting, it was a battle, a war, victory, a long fight, dropped bomb, bombshell)
Health and illness (a cancer in the department; fatal; on life support)
Animals (scratched and clawed, like a cheetah)
Fire (set ablaze, burned him)
Light and darkness (shining example, darkened her chances)
Buildings and landscape (stairway to the top, opening doors)
Building and construction
Machines and tools (hammered, working together like two gears, a fine-tuned engine; drilled him)
Game and sport (touchdown, scoring opportunities, fumbled; dropped the ball, home run, coach)
Money & economic transactions (invested in her, in the red, at great cost, cashed out)
Cooking and food (boiled over, icing on the case, bad taste in his mouth)

These are the most common sources (source domains, if you're searching for more online) for metaphors. Interestingly, the greatest political speakers of the last few decades - one Republican, one Democrat - relied heavily on metaphors and routinely drew from each and every one of these domains. That is unusual among political speakers, according to some studies. But Ronald Reagan and Barack Obama, the two politicians whose speeches have notably drawn on every single one of the core metaphor domains, had markedly higher rates of metaphor usage per speech than other leaders of comparable prominence. Across a range of speeches, according to researcher Jonathan Chateris-Black, Ronald Reagan had 479 metaphors, and Barack Obama 447 metaphors, for a rough average of about 9 ½ metaphors *for every 1000 words of speech.* Other politicians including Bill Clinton, Margaret Thatcher, Tony Blair, and both Presidents Bush, used far less and, intriguingly, were not known as particularly good speakers. Presentation has something to do with it, of course, and both Reagan and Obama spoke with great passion. But the high frequency of metaphors has been linked by many linguistic scholars to the effectiveness of their messaging. They struck a chord with ordinary people. Their words resonated. They built their presentations around concepts that people already knew and understood. Speeches are given by politicians by the bushel every single day. But these two politicians had the savvy to speak to their audiences in ways that the audiences easily understood, based on their own beliefs and values.

Conclusion

I hope you found the book useful. As I stressed throughout, the compliance or persuasion principles that comprise the PERM system are not novel. It is only their compilation into an easy to use system for closing arguments that is new. The four techniques are among roughly forty scientifically-proven methods of gaining acceptance or agreement about a product or idea. They were chosen for PERM because of their simplicity, powerful effectiveness and suitability for the restricted world of a jury trial.

Good luck, and thank you.

Jim Garrity
Ross and Rubin Publishing
New York

Made in the USA
Monee, IL
13 September 2026

62979542R00046